## DATE DUE

| | | | |
|---|---|---|---|
| DEC 1 4 198 | JAN 2 1 1985 | 49 | APR 1 0 2012 |
| JAN 4 1984 | | OCT 1 1996 FEB 2 5 2011 | |
| | OCT 1 5 1996 | | |
| FEB 15 1984 | OCT 2 3 1996 | DEC 1 2016 | |
| FEB 2 0 1984 | DEC 1 7 199 | DEC 5 2016 | |
| 2 1 1984 | MAY 2 8 1997 | | |
| | OC 26 04 | NOV 1 8 2009 | |
| DEC 3 1984 | NO 9 04 | OCT 5 2010 | |
| MAY 2 1 1984 | A 1 9 05 | OCT 1 2010 | |
| | FE 2 05 | | |
| OCT 3 1984 | AP 13 05 | | |
| FEB 31 1985 | JAN 0 8 2009 | | |
| FEB 1 6 1993 | NOV 9 2010 | | |

631.3
OLN
C.2

Olney, Ross R.
Farm giants

© THE BAKER & TAYLOR CO.

# FARM
# GIANTS

# FARM GIANTS

# by Ross R. Olney

*Atheneum*     *1982*     *New York*

# Acknowledgments

*The author would like to thank the following*
*for advice, photos and technical information*

*Blackwelder*
*M. M. Geisler, Caterpillar Tractor Co.*
*Larry Jagnow, International Harvester*
*Steve H. Kohl, J. I. Case*
*Will McCracken, Deere & Company*
*Sandy Ostbye, Steiger Tractor Company*
*Gerald L. Purser, Allis-Chalmers*

*Library of Congress Cataloging in Publication Data*

Olney, Ross Robert, Farm giants.

Includes index.
SUMMARY: Text and photos introduce the major farm
machines, their purposes, and the methods of operating each one.
1. Agricultural machinery—Juvenile literature.
[1. Agricultural machinery]    I. Title.
S675.25.046    631.3    82-1798
ISBN 0-689-30937-6    AACR2

Copyright © 1982 by Ross Olney
All rights reserved
Published simultaneously in Canada by
McClelland & Stewart, Ltd.
Composition by Dix Type Inc., Syracuse, New York
Printed and bound by
Halliday Lithograph Corporation,
West Hanover, Massachusetts
Designed by Mary M. Ahern
First Edition

# Contents

# Foreword

**F**ARMERS work very hard to grow the food we eat. They get up early in the morning. They often work until the sun goes down. They even work at night during certain times of the year to get crops planted or harvested.

There are *hundreds* of jobs to do around a farm. Farmers must feed the animals and care for them. They must repair barns and fix fences. They must keep the machines running.

The main job of most farmers is to grow crops. Today, farmers have all kinds of giant machines to help them. The machines help the farmer to work more land in less time and with fewer people. With more crops to sell the farmer can make more money. Of course, these machines are very expensive, so some of the money must go to pay for them.

This book has pictures of most of the farm giants used today. Remember, these machines are used on *big* farms and ranches. A farmer on a small farm uses smaller versions of these same machines.

A modern farm giant at work in a wheat field. Harvesting used to be done by hand, but now it is done by these great combines. (JOHN DEERE PHOTO)

# CHAPTER ONE
# Tractors

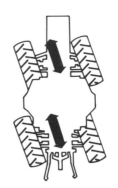

**Four-wheel grabsteering**

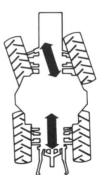

**Front wheel only**

Horsepower has replaced horses on farms. This farmer is taking a break on the steps of his huge tractor. He can steer this farm giant by turning the *front* and the *rear* wheels as shown in the diagrams. (J. I. CASE PHOTO AND DRAWING)

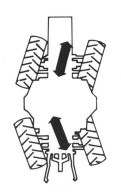

**Four-wheel coordination**

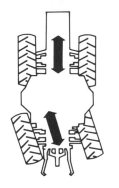

**Rear wheel only**

The tractor is the most important piece of farm equipment. It is used to tow many of the other machines the farmer uses. The farmer can also use the engine of the tractor to do work around the barn, such as lifting heavy loads. Tractors come in all sizes, from small to very large, like this one. (J. I. CASE PHOTO)

5

This tractor has a scraper on the front for use as an earth mover. Tomorrow it might be towing a plow or a disk in another field. (STEIGER TRACTOR INC. PHOTO)

The farmer looks small as she crawls up into her huge tractor. But she can control the great machine easily from the comfortable cab. (ALLIS CHALMERS PHOTO)

Some giant tractors have four-wheel drive. This means that both the front and rear wheels power the tractor. Add four more wheels, like this one, and you have *eight*-wheel drive. This tractor is also "articulated." This means it can bend in the middle for sharp turns. (JOHN DEERE PHOTO)

The same tractor bends sideways if there is a bump in the field. The engine in large tractors is often "turbocharged."

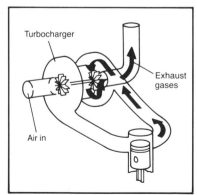

This means the force of the exhaust gases is used to force more fresh air . . . and more power . . . into the engine. (JOHN DEERE PHOTO)

9

Some farm tractors have tracks like an Army tank instead of wheels. This farmer is leveling his field near Yuba City, California. Some good farmers feel that tracks do not pack down the soil as much as wheels. (CATERPILLAR PHOTO)

Many farm equipment cabs are soundproofed and air-conditioned. They have seats that adjust the way the farmer wants them. The cabs are also pressurized so that air is always flowing *out*. *Dust* cannot get *in*. (JOHN DEERE PHOTO)

11

These huge tractors use laser beams to level a farmer's field near Visalia, California. The beams are set up around the edge of the field. The sticks on the tractors receive the beams and automatically raise or lower the blades. (CATER- PILLAR PHOTO)

# CHAPTER TWO
# **Preparing and Planting**

Farmers used to hitch up a team of horses and work for days and weeks to plow a field. Plowing is very important. The plow digs up hard ground to break it up. It softens the upper six to sixteen inches (or more) of soil. Plowing can also turn under the remains of last year's crop to kill weeds and insects. (INTERNATIONAL HARVESTER PHOTO)

Look at this ground that has been plowed. Air moves better in plowed ground. Oxygen can get down and work on organic material in the ground, releasing food for plants to grow on. (J. I. CASE PHOTO)

Plowing is done in different ways in different parts of the country, according to the type of soil and the kind of crop. This farmer is using a *moldboard* bottom plow. This is the type of plow that turns the soil over, burying last year's crop stalks. (J. I. CASE PHOTO)

A *chisel* bottom plow has steel fingers that scrape down into the soil. This breaks up the hard crust on the surface, but it doesn't turn over the soil. You can see the weeds even after this small chisel bottom plow has passed by. But this plow will do the job just fine for certain soil conditions and for certain crops. (J. I. CASE PHOTO)

15

Here is a giant chisel bottom plow in action. This farmer needs a lot of power to pull all of the steel fingers through the hard soil. (J. I. CASE PHOTO)

Farmers can plow with a series of disks. Or, as this farmer
is doing, they can further break up the soil after it has been
turned over by a moldboard bottom plow. Disking chews up
last year's crop stalks and is also a good way to mix fertilizer
into the soil before planting. (JOHN DEERE PHOTO)

This farmer is using a disk directly on the remains of last year's crop. This chews up the old crop, wheat stubble here, and also turns up the ground. (CATERPILLAR PHOTO)

Sub-soiling digs into the ground almost one *yard* deep. This really chews up the soil to get it ready for planting, but the tractor must have a great deal of power. (CATERPILLAR PHOTO)

This machine uses air pressure to plant seeds automatically. The disks cut a furrow in the prepared ground and firm the sides of the groove. Then the machine drops the seeds and covers the furrow. The last little wheel in each row presses the soil down just right. Gauges tell the farmer that everything is going well. (INTERNATIONAL HARVESTER PHOTO)

While the plants are growing, disks are run through the crops, between the rows, to keep the upper surface of the ground broken up. This is called "cultivating." Then huge machines like this come along just to spray the crops. This helps control weeds or insects that could do damage. The spraying machines also can spray fertilizer. (JOHN DEERE PHOTO)

Can you imagine a farmer towing a machine to *tear out* some of his crop? This machine thins out the crop by cutting out some of the seedlings. The others will then grow better, because they have more room. (JOHN DEERE PHOTO)

# CHAPTER THREE
# Harvesting

The whole idea of farming is to get the crop in. And farm giants do this job very well. The *combine* is the main harvesting machine. They call it this because it combines harvesting (or cutting) with threshing. Threshing is removing the grain from the stalk. The combine does both jobs, such as this corn combine is doing. Note the corn kernels in the storage tank. (JOHN DEERE PHOTO)

23

This giant combine is also set up to harvest corn. The farmer is checking the oil before he starts up the huge diesel engine. (JOHN DEERE PHOTO)

Here the same combine harvests corn in the field. The "head" or cutter can be changed to harvest row crops like corn and soybeans, or wheat and other grains. (JOHN DEERE PHOTO)

Nothing is wasted on a modern farm. This "stalker" cuts the corn stalks after the harvest. The stalks are chopped up into animal food. (JOHN DEERE PHOTO)

It is evening and time to head back to the barn. Just flip on the lights, push a button to raise the corn cutting head, and drive back to the barnyard. (ALLIS CHALMERS PHOTO)

This combine is harvesting wheat. The grain is stored in the "N6" tank and then blown out the tube to the right and into a truck that follows along beside. The chaff (the outer covering of the seed and the stems and stalks) is dropped behind the machine. (ALLIS CHALMERS PHOTO)

This combine is built to work on a hillside. But the farmer stays level over his wheat field in his comfortable cab. (ALLIS CHALMERS PHOTO)

A single combine will harvest dozens of acres in a long day's work. With a team of combines working into the night, hundreds of acres can be harvested. (JOHN DEERE PHOTO)

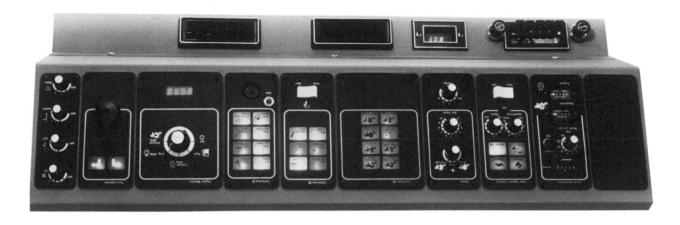

Panels such as this one inside the cab tell the farmer everything he needs to know about how his combine is working.
(ALLIS CHALMERS PHOTO)

Check this inside-out view for comfort.
The farmer can see the entire cutting
head of his Gleaner combine from his
easy chair. (ALLIS CHALMERS PHOTO)

There are special types of harvesters for special crops. This giant machine is used to pick *underground crops* such as potatos. Here it is harvesting beets in Michigan. The beets are carried into the truck by a moving belt. (JOHN DEERE PHOTO)

Tomatoes? Here is how they are harvested. They are cut and carried by moving belts to where the riding farm workers sort them into different sizes. The workers also remove any rocks or other debris that have been picked up by the machine. (BLACKWELDER PHOTO)

Gone are the days when cotton was picked by hand, then stuffed into a bag slung over the cotton picker's shoulder. These giant cotton pickers pick the cotton and store it in the huge tanks behind the cab. (JOHN DEERE PHOTO)

This boy is standing by the side of a cotton picker during lunch break on a California farm. The cotton plants slide between the cutting bars and the cotton balls are removed and blown into the storage hopper. When the hopper is full, the cotton is removed and squeezed into bales. (PHOTO BY AUTHOR)

These are "windrowers" and they are giants, indeed. They cut and lay down the hay in long rows for drying. It will be picked up by still another farm giant while it is still fresh, then stored for animal food. (JOHN DEERE PHOTO)

Don't get behind this farm giant! The machine bales hay, then flips the heavy bales into the following wagon. The force of the throw can be controlled by the man on the tractor. (JOHN DEERE PHOTO)

The farmer can choose the size of his hay bale by choosing the size of the baler. The one at the left gives him a four-by-five-foot, 850-pound bale. The one on the right makes a five-by-six-foot, 1,700-pound bale. (JOHN DEERE PHOTO)

Have you ever heard of a *round* bale of hay? That's what this farm giant makes for the farmers who want them. Just beneath the outside layer the hay stays green and healthy in all kinds of weather, just right for farm animals to eat. (JOHN DEERE PHOTO)

A "stack wagon" is towed along a windrow and the hay is picked up and compressed inside. It is packed so tightly that even a strong wind won't later tear it apart. (JOHN DEERE PHOTO)

This stack will last all winter long. The shape of the hay stack sheds rain and snow. After a full year, the hay just under the top layer is still green and good-tasting to farm animals. (JOHN DEERE PHOTO)

# Index